D0821847

After Experience is Mr. Snodgrass's first collection of poetry since his Pulitzer Prize-winning *Heart's Needle.* About *Heart's Needle,* Donald Hall wrote, "Mr. Snodgrass seems able to do almost anything and he uses his skill with tact." And William Meredith said, "Snodgrass offers us, first, a genuine subject imbued with genuine feeling and, second, a voice that is, at least much of the time, personal and distinct."

After Experience will enhance Mr. Snodgrass's reputation. In this book he continues to write poetry from direct experience as well as more objective work, amongst which is a section of poems devoted to various paintings by Vuillard, Monet, Manet, Van Gogh. The book ends with a section of translations of poems by Rilke, Rimbaud, Mörike, and others. These translations are in themselves English poetry of a high order.

BOOKS BY W. D. SNODGRASS

Poetry

HEART'S NEEDLE
AFTER EXPERIENCE

Translation

GALLOWS SONGS, by Christian Morgenstern
(in collaboration with Lore Segal)

W. D. SNODGRASS

AFTER EXPERIENCE

Poems and Translations

Harper & Row, Publishers
New York, Evanston, and London

Acknowledgments are due to the following publications in which many of these poems have appeared: *Atlantic Monthly, Burning Deck, Encounter, The Sixties* (formerly called *The Fifties*), *Harper's Magazine, The Kenyon Review, Listen, The Literary Times, The New Mexico Quarterly, Partisan Review, The Portfolio & Art News Annual, Quagga, The Quarterly Review of Literature, The Saturday Evening Post, Views, Wayne Review, William & Mary Review.* "Partial Eclipse" appeared in POETRY IN CRYSTAL, Copyright © 1963 by Steuben Glass. Translation of "True Name" by Yves Bonnefoy first appeared in *Contemporary French Poetry* edited by Aspel and Justice and published by the University of Michigan Press. Translation of "Sonnets to Orpheus" by Rainer Maria Rilke first appeared in *Reading Modern Poetry* edited by Carrier and Engel and published by Scott, Foresman, & Co. "Leaving Ithaca," "On My Child's Death," "Manet: The Execution of the Emperor Maximilian," "Edmund to Gloucester," "Takeoff," "No Use," "Green Huntsmen," and "Vuillard: The Mother and Sister of the Artist" were first published in *The Hudson Review.* "Lying Awake," "Powwow (Tama Reservation, 1949)," "Lobsters in the Window," "The Lovers Go Fly a Kite," and "Point Pelee in March" were first published in *The New Yorker.* "The Examination" was the Phi Beta Kappa ceremonial poem at Columbia University, 1961. "Autumn Scene" was the Phi Beta Kappa ceremonial poem at William and Mary College, 1966. "Edmund to Gloucester" was commissioned for the celebration of the fourth centenary of Shakespeare's birth.

FIRST EDITION

LIBRARY OF CONGRESS CATALOG CARD NUMBER: 67-22508

A-S

To My Parents

CONTENTS

I
POEMS

II
TRANSLATIONS

ACKNOWLEDGMENTS

I am most deeply grateful to Donald Hall and to George P. Elliott, for the sustenance of their friendship and the generosity of their critical intelligence. I am equally unable to give any adequate thanks to Camille.

I am much indebted to the National Endowment in the Arts for a grant and to the Corporation of Yaddo and the MacDowell Colony for periods in residence.

I

POEMS

PARTIAL ECLIPSE

Last night's eclipse, 99% complete,
seemed at times to be total because
of light mists and low-hanging clouds.
—Radio news report

Once we'd packed up your clothes
It was something to talk about:
The full moon, how it rose
Red, went pale, then went out

As that slow shadow crossed—
The way Time might erase
Its blackboard: one cheek lost,
The eyes, most of the face

Hovering dim as a ghost,
Or the dark print of some light
That seared the eyes, almost,
Yet lives in the lids, clenched tight.

But still one brilliant sliver
Stayed, worrying the eye,
Till even that would shiver,
Go sick and the whole sky—

We wished it all blank, bereft.
But no; the mists drifted on;
Something, one glint was left.
Next morning you had gone.

SEPTEMBER

In town, your friends play hide-and-seek
  In dead leaves piled by the sidewalk.
Today I hiked along the creek,
  Through dry weeds and the sharp oat stalks,

Carrying my old binoculars;
  I hoped to spot that small Green Heron
We saw together down the marsh
  This August. He'd gone off on an errand.

Then too, of course, this *is* September.
  The newts in the creek had gone, already.
I don't know where. I can't remember
  Your face or anything you said.

RECONSTRUCTIONS

This fall, we left your Grandma's
And had to leave your plant behind;
You said if no one watered it
And it would die, you didn't mind.
You mean to play the zinnia
In some sorry melodrama.

You offered me, one day, your doll
To sing songs to, bubble and nurse,
And said that was her birthday;
You reappeared then, grabbed her away,
Said just don't mess with her at all;
It was your child, yours.

And earlier this summer, how
You would tell the dog he had to "Stay!"
Then always let him sit
There, ears up, tense, all
Shivering to hear you call;
You turned and walked away.

We are like patients who rehearse
Old unbearable scenes
Day after day after day.
I memorize you, bit by bit,
And must restore you in my verses
To sell to magazines.

We keep what our times allow
And turn our grief into play.
We left you at your mother's; now
We've given the dog away.

THE FIRST LEAF

The first leaf, as we drive off,
Spins down the windshield, red;
Birds flock near the driveway.
We say what has to be said:

Autumn, winter, spring,
We'll write our usual letter;
One month for each finger.
And this makes you feel better.

We park by a transport trailer
Of bawling, white-faced cattle
That stare between the truck rails
Like men being shipped to battle,

Perhaps, in some other country,
But who will ever know?
From somewhere down the station
I hear a rooster crow.

Next year we'll hardly know you;
Still, all the blame endures.
This year you will live at our expense;
We have a life at yours,

Now I can earn a living
By turning out elegant strophes.
Your six-year teeth lie on my desk
Like a soldier's trophies.

You move off where I send you;
The train pulls down its track.
We go about our business;
I have turned my back.

MEMENTOS, 1

Sorting out letters and piles of my old
  Canceled checks, old clippings, and yellow note cards
That meant something once, I happened to find
  Your picture. *That* picture. I stopped there cold,
Like a man raking piles of dead leaves in his yard
    Who has turned up a severed hand.

Still, that first second, I was glad: you stand
  Just as you stood—shy, delicate, slender,
In that long gown of green lace netting and daisies
  That you wore to our first dance. The sight of you stunned
Us all. Well, our needs were different, then,
    And our ideals came easy.

Then through the war and those two long years
  Overseas, the Japanese dead in their shacks
Among dishes, dolls, and lost shoes; I carried
  This glimpse of you, there, to choke down my fear,
Prove it had been, that it might come back.
    That was before we got married.

—Before we drained out one another's force
  With lies, self-denial, unspoken regret
And the sick eyes that blame; before the divorce
  And the treachery. Say it: before we met. Still,
I put back your picture. Someday, in due course,
    I will find that it's still there.

MEMENTOS, 2

I found them there today
in the third-floor closet,
packed away
among our wedding gifts
under the thick deposit
of black coal dust that sifts
down with the months:
that long white satin gown
and the heavy lead-foil crown
that you wore once
when you were Queen of the May,
the goddess of our town.

That brilliant hour
you stood, exquisite, tall,
for the imperious Power
that drives and presses all
seed and the buried roots
to rise from the dead year.
I saw your hair,
the beauty that would fall
to the boy who won you. Today,
I wondered where,
in what dark, your wedding suit
lies packed away.

How proud I was to gain you!
No one could warn
me of the pride or of
the fear my love might stain you
that would turn your face to scorn—
of the fear you could not love

that would tease and haunt you
till all that made me want you
would gall you like a crown
of flowering thorn.
My love hung like a gown
of lead that pulled you down.

I saw you there once, later—
the hair and the eyes dull,
a grayness in the face—
a woman with a daughter
alone in the old place.
Yet the desire remains:
for times when the right boys sought you;
to be courted, like a girl.
I thought of our years; thought you
had had enough of pain;
thought how much grief I'd brought you;
I wished you well again.

LEAVING ITHACA

—to my plaster replica of
the Aphrodite of Melos

Lady who stands on my long writing table,
I've brought seashells and fossils; I have put
Oak leaves weathered to gray lace at your foot,
Meaning I'll go your way when I am able.

Ten years now we've been transients since my mother
Mailed you, packed in towels, when I first married.
How often you've been boxed up, shipped or carried
From house to house, from one love to another.

When we first met, you'd lost a set of toes
And both your arms. Oh everloving Lady,
You had been ruined quite enough already;
Now the children have chipped off half your nose.

My first wife tried to keep you in the attic;
Some thought your breasts just so-so and your waist,
Thick with childbearing, not for modern taste.
My father thought you lewd and flicked your buttocks.

One giddy night, blonde Susan tipped your stand—
You, true to your best style, lost your head.
You just won't learn how much smart girls will shed
This year. Well, we must both look secondhand.

Lady, we've cost each other. Still, it's been
Lovelier than I would have dared ask here:
My own house, my own woman, this whole year—
Lovelier than things will likely be again:

The handmade rough old farmhouse, out of sight
In overgrowth, in spruce and scrubby pines,
In lilac, in sumac, in the wild-grape vines,
And arbor vitae on the lawn upright;

The tulips rising from forgotten beds,
Our welcome mat springing up green in clover,
Great maples scattering their winged seeds over
The chicken houses, the abandoned sheds

And the old barn, rotten, tremulous with owls,
The unpruned orchard, rank in its own mash,
Where pheasants nest, orioles fight and flash,
And evenings, silently, the groundhog prowls.

Now, of course, we have to move again
And leave the old house roughhewn as we found it,
The wild meadows and unworked fields around it—
No doubt it would have spoiled us to remain.

We'll leave our kittens, tagged for the new tenants;
The mother cat we couldn't bear to spay;
We'll take the dog along to give away
To someone who can pay for his dependents.

We'll leave the bunting and the scarlet tanagers
Here for the ladies' clubs, for our kind neighbors
Who know enough to get more from their labors,
Meet the right people or be better managers.

Already you can see them through the trees—
Bulldozed lots where men will spend their lives
In glossy houses kept by glossy wives
That have no past or future, but will please

The company. They go for the main chance
But always save the weekend for their passions;
They dress just far enough behind the fashions
And think right thoughts. They keep it in their pants.

Lady, we are going to have another child.
Was that the one thing you could send us, Lady?
You've brought us poverty enough already,
And that goes with us. Well, we are reconciled

Almost; almost. It's not smart, I suppose,
And where do we go now? We fume and worry;
We still just can't quite make ourselves feel sorry.
You've had these troubles; you know how it goes.

We'll try to live with evils that we choose,
Try not to envy someone else's vices,
But make the most of ours. We picked our crisis;
We'll lose the things we can afford to lose

And lug away what's left in orange crates:
Our driftwood, milkweed pods and Christmas cones,
A silver spoon Grandmother left, brook stones
Our daughters painted for my paperweights,

Snapshots, letters, the gimcracks that belong
To the children, the yellowing books we've read
For bedtime, and our own secondhand bed.
And you, Lady—we're taking you along.

WHAT WE SAID

Stunned in that first estrangement,
We went through the turning woods
Where inflamed leaves sick as words
Spun, wondering what the change meant.

Half gone, our road led onwards
By barbed wire, past the ravine
Where a lost couch, snarled in vines,
Spilled its soiled, gray innards

Into a garbage mound.
We came, then, to a yard
Where tarpaper, bottles and charred
Boards lay on the trampled ground.

This had been someone's lawn.
And, closing up like a wound,
The cluttered hole in the ground
A life had been built upon.

In the high grass, cars had been.
On the leafless branches, rags
And condoms fluttered like the flags
Of new orders moving in.

We talked of the last war, when
Houses, cathedral towns, shacks—
Whole continents went into wreckage.
What fools could do that again?

Ruin on every side—
We would set our loves in order,
Surely, we told each other.
Surely. That's what we said.

TAKEOFF

This is your captain. Our air-
speed is now 360 m.p.h., our
altitude 32,000 ft. Outside your
cabin window it is 80° below zero.

We slant off toward the bay
  Miles and miles above you.
How soon things shrink away.
  I don't know whether I love you
Or what I need to say.

In one of the houses, down there
  In that rainswept city,
You curl in your bed, somewhere,
  Alone—and more's the pity.
Here, the thinned-out air

Is 80 degrees below
  And the world is far more distant
Than we'd have thought. What though
  We touched for an instant,
Opened, and could grow

Close till desire turned pure
  Gouging after some old
Grief, no love now will cure.
  Well, we were always told
Some feelings do endure.

Suppose our loves *did* cross,
  Who knows where this could finish,
What cravings we could cause?
  Still, who would dare diminish
The loveliness or the loss?

LYING AWAKE

This moth caught in the room tonight
Squirmed up, sniper-style, between
The rusty edges of the screen;
Then, long as the room stayed light,

Lay here, content, in some cornerhole.
Now that we've settled into bed
Though, he can't sleep. Overhead,
He hurls himself at the blank wall.

Each night hordes of these flutterers haunt
And climb my study windowpane;
Fired by reflection, their insane
Eyes gleam; they know what they want.

How do the petulant things survive?
Out in the fields they have a place
And proper work, furthering the race;
Why this blind fanatical drive

Indoors? Why rush at every spark,
Cigar, headlamp or railway warning
To knock off your wings and starve by morning?
And what could a moth fear in the dark

Compared with what you meet inside?
Still, he rams the fluorescent face
Of the clock, thinks that's another place
Of light and families, where he'll hide.

We'd ought to trap him in a jar,
Or come, like the white-coats, with a net
And turn him out toward living. Yet
We don't; we take things as they are.

THE PLATFORM MAN

Squat, dark as a troll,
  With a gripped wooden block
In each hand, he rolled
  Himself along the sidewalks

Or, by the 5 and 10, sat
  On that wheeled dolly, begging,
With pencils and a hat
  Laid on his thick stumps of legs.

His stare leveled with my
  Stare, when I was a child.
He felt no need to try
  Any of those wild

Stunts our tightrope clever
  Kids do on their cool new boards.
Somehow he got upstairs, over
  Curbs, somehow, through doors.

Day after day, if I went
  Past, I didn't look.
I never gave him a cent.
  After all, such luck

As he had might rub off.
  Such men better get used
To the loss—it's bad enough
  Without more things to lose.

How much could he expect?
He wouldn't as much as sing.
From sideshows, stages, lecterns,
We hear men offering

New incredible talents,
Spectacular handicaps,
Who've shaped strange arts to balance
Whatever it is they lack.

Some went too far and lost
Things he was saved from wanting—
Influence, love, applause.
I'd travel light: take nothing

Free and give no quarter.
The curse is far from done
When they've taken your daughter;
They can take your son.

VAMPIRE'S AUBADE

Why so drawn, so worn,
My dearest;
Should this sun-drenched morn
Find you so burned out and so pale?
Until now I've had no fear lest
You'd be quick to fail.

Just last night, your glowing
Cheek and breast
Entranced me, overflowing
With their young love, warm and strong.
Not to freely give your best,
Dear—you'd think that wrong.

Then rise; shine; let your laughter
Fill the air.
When I do need looking after
And there's so much to be done,
Dear, it surely isn't fair
So to hang on everyone.

Or don't you care?

LOBSTERS IN THE WINDOW

First, you think they are dead.
Then you are almost sure
One is beginning to stir.
Out of the crushed ice, slow
As the hands of a schoolroom clock,
He lifts his one great claw
And holds it over his head;
Now, he is trying to walk.

But like a run-down toy;
Like the backward crabs we boys
Splashed after in the creek,
Trapped in jars or a net,
And then took home to keep.
Overgrown, retarded, weak,
He is fumbling yet
From the deep chill of his sleep

As if, in a glacial thaw,
Some ancient thing might wake
Sore and cold and stiff
Struggling to raise one claw
Like a defiant fist;
Yet wavering, as if
Starting to swell and ache
With that thick peg in the wrist.

I should wave back, I guess.
But still in his permanent clench
He's fallen back with the mass
Heaped in their common trench
Who stir, but do not look out
Through the rainstreaming glass,
Hear what the newsboys shout,
Or see the raincoats pass.

LOOKING

What was I looking for today?
All that poking under the rugs,
Peering under the lamps and chairs,
Or going from room to room that way,
Forever up and down the stairs
Like someone stupid with sleep or drugs.

Everywhere I was, was wrong.
I started turning the drawers out, then
I was staring in at the icebox door
Wondering if I'd been there long
Wondering what I was looking for.
Later on, I think I went back again.

Where did the rest of the time go?
Was I down cellar? I can't recall
Finding the light switch, or the last
Place I've had it, or how I'd know
I didn't look at it and go past.
Or whether it's what I want, at all.

AUTUMN SCENE

In the public gardens they are walking.
    The skies appear correct and glum.
Their heels click drily; they are talking.
Behind their backs, the elms repeat some shocking
    News of what's to come.

Otherwise, the lawns like quiet.
    The beds are vacant, spaded, formal,
Where sparrows peck out a lean diet.
After July's sun-scattering splash and riot,
    It's back to gray and normal.

The gods and goddesses who stood
    Here by the sundial, enshrined,
Absurd, and eminently nude,
Are nailed into their houses of worn wood,
    Out of sight, of mind.

Even the flowers' namecards are gone.
    As if some fly-by-night affair,
Flaunting rich color through the air,
Had quietly packed its furniture, withdrawn
    Its funds, moved—who knows where?

A white gull spins in off the river
    Jeering; one tiny wave expands
Along the hedges like a shiver.
They're walking slow; somehow, they manage never
    To touch each other's hands.

A FRIEND

I walk into your house, a friend.
Your kids swarm up my steep hillsides
Or swing in my branches. Your boy rides
Me for his horsie; we pretend
Some troll threatens our lady fair.
I swing him squealing through the air
And down. Just what could I defend?

I tuck them in, sometimes, at night.
That's one secret we never tell.
Giggling in their dark room, they yell
They love me. Their father, home tonight,
Sees your girl curled up on my knee
And tells her "git"—she's bothering me.
I nod; she'd better think he's right.

Once they're in bed, he calls you "dear."
The boob-tube shows some hokum on
Adultery and loss; we yawn
Over a stale joke book and beer
Till it's your bedtime. I must leave.
I watch that squat toad pluck your sleeve.
As always, you stand shining near

Your window. I stand, Prince of Lies
Who's seen bliss; now I can drive back
Home past wreck and car lot, past shack
Slum and steelmill reddening the skies,
Past drive-ins, the hot pits where our teens
Fingerfuck and that huge screen's
Images fill their vacant eyes.

NO USE

No doubt this way is best.
No doubt in time I'd learn
To hate you like the rest
I once loved. Like an old
Shirt we unstitch and turn
Until it's all used out,
This too would turn cold.
    No doubt . . . no doubt . . .

And yet who'd dare think so
And yet dare think? We've been
Through all this; we should know
That man the gods have curst
Can ask and always win
Love, as castaways get
Whole seas to cure their thirst.
    And yet . . . and yet . . .

No use telling us love's
No use. Parched, cracked, the heart
Drains that love it loves
And still thirsts. We still care;
We're spared *that.* We're apart.
Tell me there's no excuse,
No sense to this despair. . . .
    No use . . . No use . . .

GREEN HUNTSMEN

So he has taken you, as trolls
  Snatch back their lovely own;
As if, with the twilight failing,
  Some sluggish majesty
Rose from the sour lagoon to snag you,
  Rapt as a memory, behind
The greened, grained mirror. Silence;
  The unblinking pond goes blind.

Still, in the upland meadows, green
  Huntsmen huddle around
That twitching in the drenched grass;
  They slash the testes, scatter out
Hair to the heavens' quarters,
  Guts to the yelping hounds.
Thoughtless, loose-tendoned as a dream
  And far, the untouched herd still bounds.

Here, the enormous trees stand
  Around me casting down
Their green into that lightless green
  Of lichens, duckweed, algae,
And those underwater plants that thrive
  In slime and deep disgrace.
I cannot find you. No.
  I cannot see my face.

THAT TIME

It's that time of the year.
Birds take off for the South;
My children fly back West,
The leaves fly right straight down.
And maybe, you, most dear, . . .
Maybe it's for the best.

Camouflaged like leaves,
Men ship out for the East.
Some of them come back.
Seasons return although
Men have to face the hour
The Powers turn their back.

Men get displaced. At least
It's better not despair.
Some find their place; they grow
Too warm, heavy with power,
While chillier nights advance
And things have got to go.

This was just in the air.
We knew this all along.
Sometimes you find a way.
Some get a second chance.
I . . . I once knew your mouth.
So go along, go along.

LEAVING THE MOTEL

Outside, the last kids holler
Near the pool: they'll stay the night.
Pick up the towels; fold your collar
Out of sight.

Check: is the second bed
Unrumpled, as agreed?
Landlords have to think ahead
In case of need,

Too. Keep things straight: don't take
The matches, the wrong keyrings—
We've nowhere we could keep a keepsake—
Ashtrays, combs, things

That sooner or later others
Would accidentally find.
Check: take nothing of one another's
And leave behind

Your license number only,
Which they won't care to trace;
We've paid. Still, should such things get lonely,
Leave in their vase

An aspirin to preserve
Our lilacs, the wayside flowers
We've gathered and must leave to serve
A few more hours;

That's all. We can't tell when
We'll come back, can't press claims;
We would no doubt have other rooms then,
Or other names.

POINT PELEE IN MARCH

The ice fishers' shacks and tents
  Work in off of the lake;
A few rough birds commence
  Rehearsing their old mistakes

And storm the heavens, filling
  The air with their raw cries.
The grudging creeks seem willing
  To acknowledge their own size.

Knowing how many seasons
  Folded and came to grief,
This silver birch might even
  Give us a little leaf

And the gray lawn thinks we merit
  One green tinge. Here, a row
Of stiff barberry can spare it
  To squeeze out a bud or so.

While the awnings tatter like flags,
  Now from his boarded cellar
The fat proprietor drags
  Orange benches and beach umbrellas

Where young lovers will retreat
  Behind their ice cream stand.
Come summer, I might meet
  Your eyes or take your hand.

THE LOVERS GO FLY A KITE

What's up, today, with our lovers?
  Only bright tatters—a kite
That plunges and bobs where it hovers
  At no improbable height.

It's shuddery like a hooked fish
  Or a stallion. They reel in string
And sprint, compassing their wish:
  To keep in touch with the thing.

They tear up their shirts for a tail
  In hopes that might steady
It down. Wobbling, frail,
  They think it may now be ready

And balance their hawk aloft—
  Poor moth of twigs and tissue
That would spill if one chill wind coughed,
  Dive down to tear, or to kiss you;

Yet still tugs the line they keep
  Like some exquisite sting ray
Hauled from a poisonous deep
  To explore the bright coasts of day,

Or say it's their weather ear
  Keeping the heart's patrol of
A treacherous, washed-out year,
  Searching for one sprig of olive.

What air they breathe is wrung
  With twenty subtleties;
Sharp bones of failure, hung
  In all the parkway trees;

It's enough to make you laugh—
  In these uncommitted regions
On an invisible staff
  To run up an allegiance!

REGRADUATING THE LUTE

Having gathered power and resonance
Through two years' playing, the finger board
Replaned to the warp of the living grain, then
We are ready. Keeping the strings
Tuned and under tension, we gradually
Pare away, while playing constantly,
All excess from behind the tempered face.
The way a long grief hollows the cheeks away.
Not so much as might lose
Endurance to sustain a music,
Yet until the sounding board is parchment-
thin, and the white bonestructure or a strong
Light would shine nearly through.
Until it trembles to the least touch,
Trembles to the lightest song.
By hand we slowly rub away
The preserving brilliant varnish to a soft
Old silver glow. Its voice now
Is equal to any in the world. We take it
Home to sing to or lay it on the bed.
In any place, at any time I play,
Behind this face where nobody can see
I have burned your name. To stay.

THE EXAMINATION

Under the thick beams of that swirly smoking light,
    The black robes are clustering, huddled in together.
Hunching their shoulders, they spread short, broad sleeves like night-
    Black grackles' wings; then they reach bone-yellow leather-

y fingers, each to each. And are prepared. Each turns
    His single eye—or since one can't discern their eyes,
That reflective, single, moon-pale disc which burns
    Over each brow—to watch this uncouth shape that lies

Strapped to their table. One probes with his ragged nails
    The slate-sharp calf, explores the thigh and the lean thews
Of the groin. Others raise, red as piratic sails,
    His wing, stretching, trying the pectoral sinews.

One runs his finger down the whet of that cruel
    Golden beak, lifts back the horny lids from the eyes,
Peers down in one bright eye malign as a jewel,
    And steps back suddenly. "He is anaesthetized?"

"He is. He is. Yes. Yes." The tallest of them, bent
    Down by the head, rises: "This drug possesses powers
Sufficient to still all gods in this firmament.
    This is Garuda who was fierce. He's yours for hours.

"We shall continue, please." Now, once again, he bends
    To the skull, and its clamped tissues. Into the cran-
ial cavity, he plunges both of his hands
    Like obstetric forceps and lifts out the great brain,

Holds it aloft, then gives it to the next who stands
    Beside him. Each, in turn, accepts it, although loath,

Turns it this way, that way, feels it between his hands
Like a wasp's nest or some sickening outsized growth.

They must decide what thoughts each part of it must think;
They tap at, then listen beside, each suspect lobe;
Next, with a crow's quill dipped into India ink,
Mark on its surface, as if on a map or globe,

Those dangerous areas which need to be excised.
They rinse it, then apply antiseptics to it;
Now silver saws appear which, inch by inch, slice
Through its ancient folds and ridges, like thick suet.

It's rinsed, dried, and daubed with thick salves. The smoky saws
Are scrubbed, resterilized, and polished till they gleam.
The brain is repacked in its case. Pinched in their claws,
Glimmering needles stitch it up, that leave no seam.

Meantime, one of them has set blinders to the eyes,
Inserted light packing beneath each of the ears
And calked the nostrils in. One, with thin twine, ties
The genitals off. With long wooden-handled shears,

Another chops pinions out of the scarlet wings.
It's hoped that with disuse he will forget the sky
Or, at least, in time, learn, among other things,
To fly no higher than his superiors fly.

Well; that's a beginning. The next time, they can split
His tongue and teach him to talk correctly, can give
Him opinions on fine books and choose clothing fit
For the integrated area where he'll live.

Their candidate may live to give them thanks one day.
He will recover and may hope for such success
He might return to join their ranks. Bowing away,
They nod, whispering, "One of ours; one of ours. Yes. Yes."

A CHARACTER

Summers, in hospital whites, he takes your breath away
strolling with the incredible deftness of an eland
among merchants, schoolboys at jab-and-scramble play,
waddling girls, the usual stink and bustle of the streets.
He stretches, easily, onto the balls of his feet
as if he might get soiled, or might recall an errand
and sail out like a white heron, someone from another planet,
dimension, some pure merciful visitor, reincarnate.

Asked for his rent, he hasn't the faintest comprehension,
but will pass on without so much as disapproval
of this corrupt town. His is that intense preoccupation
one sees in nuns or eighteenth century fops.
He frequents only the most fashionable of the shops
neither to buy nor sell; beyond good and evil,
he saunters along the aisles, lifting the cunningest
little things—his own by right of natural good taste.

And hasn't he, after all, the right—no, almost the duty—
to take care that such fine things are not neglected
in the hands of those who couldn't appreciate them truly?
And after all, if you think what he has suffered,
it is no more than just that he should recover
the few small things he has been able to collect?
Surely a man needs some haven, some small fortress
against manifest vulgarity and worldliness?

His throw rugs and furniture are all in whites;
lately, he's done the walls white like a physician's
consultation room. He sits up languishing, nights,
cleaning his nails, or lies down to inspect his injuries
since, though he lives immaculately, he's
developed a strange susceptibility to lesions
apparently of some old wound he's liable to forget.
He thinks the world is his scab and picks at it.

FLASH FLOOD

The worst is over; the people
are all glad
to show you where it passed, scattering
paving bricks like handbills, elbowed
STOP
signs into respectful
attitudes, then filched the smug
porch off a house.
They lead you to a black hole where
it broke straight
through one block wall of a basement, then
as if appalled by something found in there,
broke back out through the opposite wall.
They will recite
the history of its progress:
its small beginnings in the hills; down
what gulleys it had gathered mud and power,
gathered rock, stumps, dead trees; gathering body
parts and boulders, engines, armchairs, train wheels, gathering
down into the town.
They argue over who first
spotted it, bubbling out of sewers;
recognized its stench; who heard it, angering
back of the welding shops and car barns; argue, finally,
where had it clambered over the creek banks, rioting
down their stunned streets, irresistibly splintering
the goods they had used their
lives collecting. For years
of skimping, hard work,
jockeying for position; for all
their small, reluctant, timorous swindlings;

for their dedication—this
is their reward. They talk about it
with such pride, you'd think
it was their own.
Think back how the orderlies danced while
bombs crazed their bunker
and the Third Reich died.
Think of the Thirties—of all those
who saw their lives totter and
falter and
go under, finally;
then began to live. Who
would not like to kick
some pretty girl?
The firemen clump around in their boots, now,
on one of the porches, talking
to the young Italian, loud, who owns it,
whom everybody watches;
he has achieved, at last, celebrity of a kind—
his kitchen departed like an excursion steamer;
he clutches his shirtfront like some short-legged Oedipus
and seems, for once, one with his destiny.
Meantime, his neighbors who have not, these many months,
found time to address each other
saunter about with coffee and extra bedding;
surprised as refugees, they may
shake hands; or will walk together, like prisoners
out for exercise. They watch
three tow trucks strain to resurrect the bones
of next year's Chevrolet, junked in the creek.
Isn't it terrible, they ask. Their eyes
are glittering with the flares and searchlights.
Awful, they say. And they may stay up, now,
probably, talking, half the night.

EDMUND TO GLOUCESTER

That you are blind, I always had admitted;
Got diddled gladly in one game or another.
If you are led about by that half-witted
Competence, my legitimate half brother,

There's nothing new. The sweet cunt of virtue,
That was you. Obscurity was your vice,
And who's to say your blindness ever hurt you
Much? For a man who had no use for eyes,

You made out. They tell me you called my name
In pain. The same name you gave me. I knew
No word for you. Nor you. Holding no claim,
I kept my breath. I never called to you,

Not even now when every farmer's dog
Wails your wet track. You? Oh, you'll lose our spies
As you lost me. Dark, tender as a fog,
You would dissolve in considerate soft lies,

Shadowy and plausible as a ghost,
Until I could pass through you like the air
I breathe. I breathed you in, each breath, but lost
Touch, could not touch you, hold you, anywhere.

Today, we touched you. So I accept your title,
Your legacy. You may go. Should I go free
To pogue this bitched world, I ask no requital.
At least, you will not need to look at me.

"AFTER EXPERIENCE TAUGHT ME . . ."

After experience taught me that all the ordinary
Surroundings of social life are futile and vain;

> I'm going to show you something very
> Ugly: someday, it might save your life.

Seeing that none of the things I feared contain
In themselves anything either good or bad

> What if you get caught without a knife;
> Nothing—even a loop of piano wire;

Excepting only in the effect they had
Upon my mind, I resolved to inquire

> Take the first two fingers of this hand;
> Fork them out—kind of a "V for Victory"—

Whether there might be something whose discovery
Would grant me supreme, unending happiness.

> And jam them into the eyes of your enemy.
> You have to do this hard. Very hard. Then press

No virtue can be thought to have priority
Over this endeavor to preserve one's being.

> Both fingers down around the cheekbone
> And setting your foot high into the chest

No man can desire to act rightly, to be blessed,
To live rightly, without simultaneously

You must call up every strength you own
And you can rip off the whole facial mask.

Wishing to be, to act, to live. He must ask
First, in other words, to actually exist.

And you, whiner, who wastes your time
  Dawdling over the remorseless earth,
What evil, what unspeakable crime
  Have you made your life worth?

EXORCISM

Out, out, you Dullard in the nerves,
Gray brinkman, tingling through the blood,
Numb-fingered, dulled in the taste bud,
Who can't eat cake, would not dare kiss,
So Chickensteers around Love's curves
Teasing the intimate abyss.

Begone, Goldfinder of the groin,
Old influence-monger in the heart,
Who knows the capitalistic art
Of making scarce whatever's worth
Desire, and pays lust's famine coin
To mine the fool's veins of his earth.

And you, Nixmaster of the tongue,
Soft wordsman, scrambling in the mind,
Unsilent Quaker who can find
True facts belying your own doubt
Till all walls fall; ruler among
The ruins of affection; out!

INQUEST

Under the lamp your hands do not seem red.
What if the vicious histories didn't lie
And, in good time, might cover you with shame?—
You seldom hope to see yourself as dead.

How can you guess what vices on your head
Might shine like dead wood for some distant eye?
Of course you have your faults; you make no claim
To sainthood, but your hands do not look red.

It's no crime to be envied or well fed;
You aimed at no man's life. Who would deny
Yours is the human and the normal aim?
You scarcely want to see yourself as dead.

Only last week the commentators said
Not even foreign generals need die
For circumstantial crimes. You would proclaim
Your own guilt if you saw your own hands red.

If you were hungry, who'd give up his bread
Without a fight? A person has to try
To feed himself; earn his own wealth and fame;
Nobody wants to see himself as dead.

Still, men go back to wars. They're not misled
By the old lies. They know the reasons why.
When you can't praise the world your world became
And see no place where your own hands are red,

It must be someone, then—how have they fled
The justice you had hoped you could apply?
You've hanged your enemies, shown up their game,
So now you don't dare see yourself as dead

And things lose focus. You can lie in bed
Repeating Men do starve. Their children cry.
They really cry. They do not cry your name.
Go back to sleep, your hands do not feel red.

Or sit in some dark newsreel to be led
Through barbed wire and the white dead piled boot-high.
Your palms sweat; you feel just about the same.
Your last hope is to see yourself as dead

And yet you did not bleed when those were bled.
The humans carry knives. "It is not I!"
The screen goes blank, you see no one to blame.
Till you endure to see yourself as dead
Your blood in your own hands would not seem red.

A VISITATION

Just as you carried out a policy of not wanting to share the earth with the Jewish people . . . (as though you and your superiors had any right to determine who should and who should not inhabit the world), we find that no member of the human race can be expected to want to share the earth with you.
—Hannah Arendt on Eichmann

At my window, I pull the curtains wide
On the Detroit night. So; it's you, again,
Old ghost? Not left once since the day you died?

    I am faithful, shivering still and pale,
    Streaked yet by traffic lights, waiting outside
    Like the poor dead soldier in some folktale

The Jews, your jailers, couldn't bear to face
Your dutiful Jewish face, in their jail,
On TV, postered, every public place,

    Come to his true love's window, wanting in
    To ask, now their love's final, love's embrace.
    I am true to you; I have always been.

Each usual nightmare. Taking that excuse
You gave to wipe out their (and your own) kin,
They hanged you. So; they've turned you loose.

    My truth enraged them. *You*, perhaps, don't need
    Someone to outcast, loathe, some way to lose
    Track of man's deceit, man's violence, greed—

When were you half so slippery, so alive
As now you're dead? You prowl the world's face, freed
To trace your own types, threaten them, connive . . .

Take me in. Secure me. Once, your own hand
Held a nightstick, .45 and sheath knife;
You've chained men to a steel beam on command.

This last, I admit. I can scarcely claim
To be my brother's keeper on so grand
A scale as yours. In a full lifetime's shame

Luck, friend, not character. We took the parts
Our time and place allowed. You played the game;
There's something beats the same in opposed hearts.

Philosophy's still your crime: the abstract
Gray lie, the sweet cliché that still imparts
Its drugged glow through the brain. The unsung fact

Who called his weakness, love? His long rage, lust?
Who called his worst lusts, honesty? Our days exact
From you, as from me, the deep faults they must.

Proves all the more cause I should keep you there—
How subtle all that chokes us with disgust
Moves in implacably to rule us, unaware.

My own love, you're all I could wish to be.
Close your eyes—I'll just wander off somewhere.
Or watch the way your world moves—you can look through me.

A FLAT ONE

Old Fritz, on this rotating bed
For seven wasted months you lay
Unfit to move, shrunken, gray,
No good to yourself or anyone
But to be babied—changed and bathed and fed.
At long last, that's all done.

Before each meal, twice every night,
We set pads on your bedsores, shut
Your catheter tube off, then brought
The second canvas-and-black-iron
Bedframe and clamped you in between them, tight,
Scared, so we could turn

You over. We washed you, covered you,
Cut up each bite of meat you ate;
We watched your lean jaws masticate
As ravenously your useless food
As thieves at hard labor in their chains chew
Or insects in the wood.

Such pious sacrifice to give
You all you could demand of pain:
Receive this haddock's body, slain
For you, old tyrant; take this blood
Of a tomato, shed that you might live.
You had that costly food.

You seem to be all finished, so
We'll plug your old recalcitrant anus
And tie up your discouraged penis
In a great, snow-white bow of gauze.
We wrap you, pin you, and cart you down below,
Below, below, because

Your credit has finally run out.
On our steel table, trussed and carved,
You'll find this world's hardworking, starved
Teeth working in your precious skin.
The earth turns, in the end, by turn about
And opens to take you in.

Seven months gone down the drain; thank God
That's through. Throw out the four-by-fours,
Swabsticks, the thick salve for bedsores,
Throw out the diaper pads and drug
Containers, pile the bedclothes in a wad,
And rinse the cider jug

Half-filled with the last urine. Then
Empty out the cotton cans,
Autoclave the bowls and spit pans,
Unhook the pumps and all the red
Tubes—catheter, suction, oxygen;
Next, wash the empty bed.

—All this Dark Age machinery
On which we had tormented you
To life. Last, we collect the few
Belongings: snapshots, some odd bills,
Your mail, and half a pack of Luckies we
Won't light you after meals.

Old man, these seven months you've lain
Determined—not that you would live—
Just to not die. No one would give
You one chance you could ever wake
From that first night, much less go well again,
Much less go home and make

Your living; how could you hope to find
A place for yourself in all creation?—
Pain was your only occupation.
And pain that should content and will
A man to give it up, nerved you to grind
Your clenched teeth, breathing, till

Your skin broke down, your calves went flat
And your legs lost all sensation. Still,
You took enough morphine to kill
A strong man. Finally, nitrogen
Mustard: you could last two months after that;
It would kill you then.

Even then you wouldn't quit.
Old soldier, yet you must have known
Inside the animal had grown
Sick of the world, made up its mind
To stop. Your mind ground on its separate
Way, merciless and blind,

Into these last weeks when the breath
Would only come in fits and starts
That puffed out your sections like the parts
Of some enormous, damaged bug.
You waited, not for life, not for your death,
Just for the deadening drug

That made your life seem bearable.
You still whispered you would not die.
Yet in the nights I heard you cry
Like a whipped child; in fierce old age
You whimpered, tears stood on your gun-metal
Blue cheeks shaking with rage

And terror. So much pain would fill
Your room that when I left I'd pray
That if I came back the next day
I'd find you gone. You stayed for me—
Nailed to your own rapacious, stiff self-will.
You've shook loose, finally.

They'd say this was a worthwhile job
Unless they tried it. It is mad
To throw our good lives after bad;
Waste time, drugs, and our minds, while strong
Men starve. How many young men did we rob
To keep you hanging on?

I can't think we did *you* much good.
Well, when you died, none of us wept.
You killed for us, and so we kept
You, because we need to earn our pay.
No. We'd still have to help you try. We would
Have killed for you today.

THE MEN'S ROOM IN THE COLLEGE CHAPEL

Here, in the most Unchristian basement
of this "fortress for the Christian mind,"
they close these four gray walls, shut out shame,
and scribble of sex and excrement,
draw bestial pictures and sign their name—
the old, lewd defiance of mankind.

The subversive human in his cell—
burn his vile books, stamp out his credo,
lock him away where no light falls,
and no live word can go back to tell
where he's entombed like Monte Cristo—
still, he'll carve his platform in the walls.

In need, men have painted the deep caves
to summon their animal, dark gods;
even the reviled, early Christians
prayed in catacombs to outlawed Good,
laid their honored dead and carved out graves
with pious mottos of resistance.

This is the last cave, where the soul
turns in its corner like a beast
nursing its wounds, where it contemplates
vengeance, how it shall gather to full
strength, what lost cause shall it vindicate,
returning, masterless and twisted.

POWWOW

They all see the same movies.
  They shuffle on one leg,
    Scuffing the dust up,
  Shuffle on the other.
They are all the same:
  A Sioux dance to the spirits;
  A war dance by four Chippewa;
  A Dakota dance for rain;
    We wonder why we came.
Even tricked out in the various braveries—
  Black buffalo tassels, beadwork, or the brilliant
  Feathers at the head, at the buttocks—
Even in long braids and the gaudy face-paints,
    They all dance with their eyes turned
  Inward—like a woman nursing
A sick child she already knows
  Will die. For the time, she nurses it,
  All the same. The loudspeakers shriek;
    We leave our bleacher seats to wander
  Among the wikiups and lean-tos
In search for hot dogs. The Indians
    Are already packing; have
  Resumed green dungarees and khaki—
  Castoff combat issues of World War II.
    (Only the Iroquois do not come here—
They work in structural steel; they have a contract
    Building the United Nations
  And Air Force installations for our future wars.)
These, though, have dismantled their hot-dog stand
    And have to drive all night
To jobs in truck stops and all-night filling stations.

We ask directions and
They scuttle away from us like moths.
Past the trailers,
Beyond us, one tepee is still shining
Over all the rest. Inside, circled by a ring
Of children, in the glare
Of one bare bulb, a shrunken fierce-eyed man
Squats at his drum, all bones and parchment,
While his dry hands move
On the drumhead, always drumming, always
Raising his toothless drawn jaw to the light
Like a young bird drinking, like a chained dog,
Howling his tribe's song for the restless young
Who wander in and out.
Words of such great age,
Not even he remembers what they mean.
We tramp back to our car,
Then nearly miss the highway, squinting
Through red and yellow splatterings on the windshield—
The garish and beautiful remains
Of grasshoppers and dragonflies
That go with us; that do not live again.

PLANTING A MAGNOLIA

A mystery of a kind:

The little drab bulldozer crawling to the curb,
Struggling like some crocodile, up,
Over, out of the old slime, onto our
Parking, across the frost-hard lawn
To the clay pit near our house—
Balancing, precarious, in its square jaws
(Like a cat its kitten or a fox some prize white goose)
Our own magnolia tree.
We settle it, easy, into a sort of grave,
Slice down the root clump and trample in
Ripe leaf rot and the mellowed topsoil of its last field.
We wire it, each way, like a TV
And have installed this
Thing more ancient than our shorelines.
And we can call it ours.

Spirited in winter sleep, it may waken
Here, and may never know.
Those roots, coiled
In the cold dark, loosed
From their burlap shrouds, what do they
Dream? What do they portend? They have come
Far. Once they were forests
In tropical Alaska,
Covered whole continents vanished undersea.

Magnolia has so much to reconsider;
Put up with horned, hawk-face
Lizards alighting in its boughs; was used to
Toothed birds, short-bodied, taller than a man.

It stood through the Age of the Great Dying:
While the seas turned cold to Portheus;
Mosasaur, plesiosaur sank into neglect;
And on the land, its old
Familiars—triceratops pasturing
The ancestral ferns, tyrannosaur the king flesh-tearer—
Perished with their successes and were gone.

It stands like a flagstaff, waiting
To declare itself.
It stood. They stand. And this
We can call ours.

Whatever warmth its dreams
Foresee, it does
Not think of us. Still, the tractor tracks
Are fading; we have reinstated, some few years,
Our lawn as we would wish it. We park
Our Volkswagen beneath its serpent boughs.
Come springtime, under branches
Leafless yet in full bloom, we will walk
Our pretty wives, seeking that scent, some memory;
Might even show our grandchildren—if we
Still live here; if the tree survives—
Its long lewd buds, dangling,
And the blown flowers, white as flakburst,
Broad as women's faces, that will open as carelessly as stars
Or cancer cells that swim into the eyepiece,
That will excite us, without hope,
Returning in the rumors of
Obscene blunt beauty that surrounds
And will survive us.
Before it dies.

MATISSE: "The Red Studio"

There is no one here.
But the objects: they are real. It is not
As if he had stepped out or moved away;
There is no other room and no
Returning. Your foot or finger would pass
Through, as into unreflecting water
Red with clay, or into fire.
Still, the objects: they are real. It is
As if he had stood
Still in the bare center of this floor,
His mind turned in in concentrated fury,
Till he sank
Like a great beast sinking into sands
Slowly, and did not look up.
His own room drank him.
What else could generate this
Terra cotta raging through the floor and walls,
Through chests, chairs, the table and the clock,
Till all environments of living are
Transformed to energy—
Crude, definitive and gay.
And so gave birth to objects that are real.
How slowly they took shape, his children, here,
Grew solid and remain:
The crayons; these statues; the clear brandybowl;
The ashtray where a girl sleeps, curling among flowers;
This flask of tall glass, green, where a vine begins
Whose bines circle the other girl brown as a cypress knee.
Then, pictures, emerging on the walls:
Bathers; a landscape; a still life with a vase;
To the left, a golden blonde, lain in magentas with flowers
        scattering like stars;

Opposite, top right, these terra cotta women, living, in
 their world of living's colors;
Between, but yearning toward them, the sailor on his red
 café chair, dark blue, self-absorbed.
These stay, exact,
Within the belly of these walls that burn,
That must hum like the domed electric web
Within which, at the carnival, small cars bump and turn,
Toward which, for strength, they reach their iron hands:
Like the heavens' walls of flame that the old magi could see;
Or those ethereal clouds of energy
From which all constellations form,
Within whose love they turn.
They stand here real and ultimate.
But there is no one here.

VUILLARD: "The Mother and Sister of the Artist"

(Instructions for the Visit)

Admire, when you come here, the glimmering hair
Of the girl; praise her pale
Complexion. Think well of her dress
Though that is somewhat out of fashion.
Don't try to take her hand, but smile for
Her hesitant gentleness.
Say the old woman is looking strong
Today; such hardiness. Remark,
Perhaps, how she has dressed herself black
Like a priest, and wears that sufficient air
That does become the righteous.
As you approach, she will push back
Her chair, shove away her plate
And wait,
Sitting squat and direct, before
The red mahogany chest
Massive as some great
Safe; will wait,
By the table and her greasy plate,
The bone half-chewed, her wine half-drained;
She will wait. And fix her steady
Eyes on you—the straight stare
Of an old politician.
Try once to meet her eyes. But fail.
Let your sight
Drift—yet never as if hunting for
The keys (you keep imagining) hung
By her belt. (They are not there.)
Watch, perhaps, that massive chest—the way
It tries to lean
Forward, toward her, till it seems to rest
Its whole household's weight
Of linens and clothing and provisions

All on her stiff back.
It might be strapped there like the monstrous pack
Of some enchanted pedlar. Dense, self-contained,
Like mercury in a ball,
She can support this without strain,
Yet she grows smaller, wrinkling
Like a potato, parched as dung;
It cramps her like a fist.
Ask no one why the chest
Has no knobs. Betray
No least suspicion
The necessities within
Could vanish at her
Will. Try not to think
That as she feeds, gains
Specific gravity,
She shrinks, light-
less as the world's
Hard core
And the per-
spective drains
In her.
Finally, above all,
You must not ever see,
Or let slip one hint you can see,
On the other side, the girl's
Cuffs, like cordovan restraints;
Forget her bony, tentative wrist,
The half-fed, worrying eyes, and how
She backs out, bows, and tries to bow
Out of the scene, grows too ethereal
To make a shape inside her dress
And the dress itself is beginning already
To sublime itself away like a vapor
That merges into the empty twinkling
Of the air and of the bright wallpaper.

MANET: "The Execution of the Emperor Maximilian"

"Aim well, muchachos; aim right
here," he pointed to his heart.
With face turned upward, he
waited, grave but calm.

These dapper soldiers, seen shooting the Emperor
Just now, stand with heels in, toes out, like ballet girls
But not so tense. Chiefly, we're forced to be aware
How splendid their spats and long white saber-holsters
Gleam. They should deduce this is some crucial affair
In view of their natty uniforms and dress gear,
Yet one of them has turned up late, naturally,
For this, which should be the true peak of his career.
He stands aside, cocking his rifle, carefully.
Still, politics may not mean much to him. Perhaps,
Since he looks less like a penguin or some old gaudy
Dressform, since he sports a white band on a red cap,
Who knows?—he may be an officer who'll give the body
The *coup de grâce.* All the grace, themselves, they could conceive,
The men peer down their long sight lines like some long shot
At billiards—some shot men might hope they could achieve
Yet they would scarcely be disgraced if they should not.

Miramón and Mejía fell at once.
A second volley was required for
Maximilian who had wished to be
shot in the body so that his
mother might see his face.

Scumbly, vague, the half-formed heads of these peasants stare
Up over the background, which is a flat rock wall.
Some yawn, some sprawl on their elbows, and some rest their
Heads on their crossed arms. They peer down like men gone dull
With heat and flies watching some tenth-rate matadors
Practice, or angels bored with all these martyrs. True,
One waves and does look like he's yelling, yet of course
That might mean triumph, outrage, or mere shock. Who
Will ever know? Maybe he thinks he knows someone
Or just wants it known he's here. Caught by the drums
And dress gear, they don't even know the names; they wait
For marvels, for a sign. Surely someone must come
Declare significance, solve how these things relate
To freedom, to their life's course, to eternity.
Random and dusty, their clustering faces are
Crumbled like rocks in the wall, from which they could be
An outgrowth—cool, distant, irrelevant as stars.

The mutilated body was given full funereal honors by the Hapsburgs, whose general downfall it prefigured. On the place of execution, moreover, was erected a small chapel to further his remembrance on earth and his forgiveness in heaven.

Still, for Maximilian, all perspective lines
End in this flat rock wall. Some may find, in the distance,
An inkling of quiet streams, or pine-shadowed lanes;
Just the same, we're cut off from all true hope of vistas
As men down a mine-shaft. The peasants, too, detached,
Held back of this blank wall from their Emperor's passion;
And the soldiers, though close, we know their aim goes past
Their victims, each fixed in his own plane of existence,
His own style—though they die, each in his own style and fashion.
And if their Emperor holds his appointed place,

He's bleached out like some child's two-penny crucifixion;
  Stands in an impartial iconoclastic light
That will not hint where you might best direct your sight—
  At the unspotlighted center, just this blank space
That rifles cross; elsewhere, a baffling contradiction
  Of shadows as if each man smuggled strange forces
Into Mexico, and moved from his own light sources. . . .

When the fraudulent French plebiscite failed to convince Maximilian he had been elected by the peons, Napoleon threatened to offer the crown to some other candidate.

. . . Yet for Maximilian, who hoped he could unite
  The Old World and the New under one ordinance—
Unfortunately his own—bind the Divine Right
  Of Hapsburgs with half-chewed liberal sentiments,
Link the True Church to the freely divisive mind,
  Shape a fixed aim from all his own diversities,
Who in his wardrobe joined all the races of mankind;
  For Maximilian, whose wife Carlotta endured
A lifetime mad with loss (or with some love disease
  He'd brought her from Brazil) confined to a convent
Where, though losing her worst fears, she always referred
  To him as Emperor of all the Firmament;
The Emperor who dreamed that one day he might stand
  At the top of some broad magnificent staircase
Vouchsafing from that height of infinite command
  One smile of infinite condescension and grace
On the human beings gathered around its base. . . .

It was as if some ne'er-do-well had found at last his true vocation; as martyr and sacrificial victim, he has seldom been surpassed.

. . . Still, for Maximilian . . . still, for the man who stands
  In the midst of his own life—or, to be exact,
Off to one side of his dying—he holds together
  Just these two who chose death with him; he holds their hands.
And they're almost obscured by the smoke. Then, in fact,
  Which IS the man? No doubt he should stand at the center,
Yet who gets shot in a frock coat and sombrero?
  In that man's bland face we see nothing, not that firm
Nobility which we demand, and *do* discern
  In this stranger by the wall, or can find elsewhere
Only in this bearded soldier of whom we know
  Nothing. Who knows? Perhaps it's this one, standing there
Spread-legged, whose clenched free hand flaps up like a doll's,
  Whose face twists upward in effort or possibly
Pain, as his chest's opened out by the rifleballs,
  His brain unties, atoms start hurtling out, blind, free,
And he, whoever he was, is all finished being.

Born, July 6, 1832; brother of
Franz Josef I, Emperor of Austria.
1854, naval administrator; 1857,
viceroy to the Lombardo-Venetian
kingdom; 1864, Emperor of Mexico.
Died, 1867.

MONET: "Les Nymphéas"

The eyelids glowing, some chill morning.
O world half-known through opening, twilit lids
Before the vague face clenches into light;
O universal waters like a cloud,
Like those first clouds of half-created matter;
O all things rising, rising like the fumes
From waters falling, O forever falling;
Infinite, the skeletal shells that fall, relinquished,
The snowsoft sift of the diatoms, like selves
Downdrifting age upon age through milky oceans;
O slow downdrifting of the atoms;
O island nebulae and O the nebulous islands
Wandering these mists like falsefires, which are true,
Bobbing like milkweed, like warm lanterns bobbing
Through the snowfilled windless air, blinking and passing
As we pass into the memory of women
Who are passing. Within those depths
What ravening? What devouring rage?
How shall our living know its ends of yielding?
These things have taken me as the mouth an orange—
That acrid sweet juice entering every cell;
And I am shared out. I become these things:
These lilies, if these things are water lilies
Which are dancers growing dim across no floor;
These mayflies; whirled dust orbiting in the sun;
This blossoming diffused as rushlights; galactic vapors;
Fluorescence into which we pass and penetrate;
O soft as the thighs of women;
O radiance, into which I go on dying . . .

VAN GOGH: "The Starry Night"

Only the little
town
remains beyond
all shock and dazzle
only this little
still
stands calm.

Row on row, the gray frame cottages, sheds
And small barns of an old Dutch town. Brownish-red
Houses with stepped gables and with high stoops,
With white or yellow doors. Plane over plane,
The angled roofs, receding, old as a memory
what flowers were blossoming, how the fruit
trees bore; had the nightingale been heard
yet; the text of Father's sermon
Edge over edge, slate roofs ascending
Like the planes of a determined head,
Like stone stairs converging, step by step,
To its still dead-center, hurricane's eye,
This village chapel tiny as a child's toy
And as far
There is something about Father
narrow-minded, icy-cold, like iron
Face by face, its quartz-blue
Salients upholding that slim spire into
The sky's rush, keen as your mother's needle
Pricking the horizon, mast firm in breaking
Waters, some lighthouse
How could I possibly be in any way of any
use to anyone? I am good for something!
where there shines
No light.

Overhead: suns; stars; blind
tracers bursting; pustules;
swamp mouths of old violence
Metaphysics
cannot hold the dizzying heavens'
shock *chaos in a goblet*
outspattering:
eleven fixed stars; one sunburst
moon. Mid-sky, mid-spasm,
the spiral galaxy
tumbling in trails of vapor like the high
gods on Garganos
L'Art
pour L'Art . . . L'Energie pour L'Energie
when the holy ground burst
into flower and a
golden dew fell around, ethereal
first mists, thin
dusts gathering into
force and matter,
Chaos contains no glass
of our caliber
fusing
destroying
burning to be whole.

Giotto and Cimabue live in an obeliscal society, solidly framed, architecturally constructed

Plane over plane, the village roofs in order,
Row on row, the dark walls of a town,
One by one, the ordered lives contained
Like climbers huddled to a rock ledge, pigs
Snuffling their trough, rooting at their dam.
Every individual a stone and
the stones clung together

Between the houses, fruit trees, or narrow
Lanes beneath the eaves-troughs and the dark
Shrubs; in back, laid out side by side,
The kitchen gardens with their heavy odors
Where dew sits chilly on the cabbage leaves
And a bird might sing
And if no actual obelisk of too
pyramidal a tragedy, no rain of frogs
Down those dark lanes you cannot see
A lantern moving or a shadow sway,
No dog howls, and your ear will never know
The footfall of some prowler, some lover's tread,
Some wanderer, long gone,
four great crises when I did not know what
I said, what I wanted, even what I did,
who cannot return.

the hollow dreams of revolutionaries . . .
they would wail in despair if once they
forgot the easy satisfaction of their
instincts, raising them to the unappeased
sufferings of the passions.

Behind: blue mountains rising,
range over range over range,
Sometimes, just as waves break
on sullen, hopeless cliffs
earth's crust
upthrusting its salt mass against
the sky; ton on broken ton of stone,
the black earth hovering over,
I feel a storm of
desire to embrace something
the ragged crests lumbering in,
murderous as the seasons,
bluer than the years, *Painting*

and much screwing are not
compatible; man relentless
as a crowd pounds, blood
hammering the walls.
becomes ambitious as soon as he
becomes impotent.
Its feathery surf,
first spies,
already washing up around
the gray outbuildings and the orchards
to embrace something, a woman, a sort
of domestic hen
a spume of ancient
vacuum shuddering to reclaim
its child;
so pale the
groves of olives, gardens
of agony, frothing about
its feet in foam.

In spring, a caged bird feels strongly
there is something he should be doing.
But what was it? He gets vague ideas.
The children say, but he has *everything*
he wants.

Down those dark streets which you can never see
Shines just this much of light:
Eleven windows and one opened door—crystals
Under tons of ore, clear garnets, warm;
Through those windows you can never see, and yet
You always wonder who is waking there
Sitting up late over a pipe, sitting, holding
Some pious, worn book between worn hands,
Who sits up late together talking, talking
The night away, planning the garden for

Next year, the necessary furnitures,
   Who may be working, shredding the cabbages,
Darning some coarse fabric by a hanging lamp,
   Who may have gotten out of bed to calm
Their children fitfully sleeping, each
   In his own bed, one by one another,
Who goes to curry and bed down the patient beasts
   Warm in their old pens. But nothing moves
In those dark streets which you can never see,
   No one is walking or will ever walk there
Now, and you will never know

Before: one black tree
between you and
the town: one cypress mocks
the thin blue spire, licking up
like flame—the green metabolism
of this forest sword
that drives you from the town.
I have sown a little garden of poppies,
sweet peas and mignonette. Now we must
wait and see what comes of it.
Still, though, the little town, how peacefully
It lies under the watchful eyes of that
Fierce heaven.
And the poor baby, too, whom I had
cared for as if he were my own
Nothing moves there yet, yet
How separate, how floating like a raft, like
Seaweed drifting outward on the tide, already
Dim, half gone,
We take death to reach a star,
diminishing into
Some middle distance of the past.
some canvases that will retain their
calm even in the catastrophe.

And still so calm
and still
so still

Zóó beeη kan gaan.

[This poem contains many quotations from Van Gogh's letters and ends with his last words. This phrase could mean, "This is the way to go," "I'd like to die like this," or "I want to go home."]

II

TRANSLATIONS

CHANSON: "SI VOUS N'AVEZ . . ."

—Victor Hugo

If you do not have anything
To tell me, why do you come so near?
Why fashion me a smile I fear
Would turn the head of any king?
If you do not have anything
To tell me, why do you come so near?

If you have not one word to say
Then, always, why do you press my hand?
About the dream, angelic and
Tender, you're dreaming on your way,
If you have not one word to say
Then, always, why do you press my hand?

If you wish only that I fly
Why are you always passing here?
At any time I see you, I
Tremble; it is my joy, my fear.
If you wish only that I fly
Why are you always passing here?

EL DESDICHADO

—Gérard de Nerval

I am the shadowed, the widowed, the disconsolate,
The Prince of Aquitania whose tower is abolished;
My single star is dead—my constellated lute
Bears only the black sun from "Melancholy."

You that, in my night of tombs, brought consolation,
Give me Posilipo, the Italian sea, again;
The flower that comforted my heart in desolation,
The trellis where the roses marry to the vine.

Am I Amor or Phoebus . . . Lusignan or Biron?
On my forehead, still, the queen's kiss holds its fire.
I've dreamed within the grotto of the swimming siren;

I have crossed over Acheron, triumphant, twice,
And modulated, one by one, on Orpheus' lyre
Sighs of the saints and the damned spirits' cries.

GOLDEN VERSES

—Gérard de Nerval

Man, Free thinker, did you think no one but Man
Thinks—in a world where life, from all things, bursts?
How freely you dispose the forces you command;
In your councils you lack only the universe.

Revere that restless spirit stirring in the beasts;
That soul, opening to Nature, which is each flower;
That mystery of love which in each metal sleeps.
All things perceive. Over your life, all things have power.

Beware; an eye watches you from the wall that's blind.
Even to matter itself, there is a voice assigned.
Never force it to serve some impious cause.

In some obscure creature, often, a god lies hidden;
And like a nascent eye, covered by its lid,
Under the surfaces of stones, pure spirit grows.

MEMORY

—Arthur Rimbaud

I.

Clear water; like salt in the teardrops of a child,
Whiteness of women's flesh assaulting the sun's light;
Silks of pennons, massed, and as lilies undefiled,
Under walls some Maid once held, their defending knight.

Games of the angels . . . No—this gold stream, on the march,
Stirs arms, heavy, black, chill above all, through grass. She,
Gloomy, with blue sky for her bed's blue canopy,
Draws curtains—shadows of the hills and of the arch.

II.

Ha! clear bouillon reaches, simmering over rocks.
This water furnishes unto its waiting beds
A bottomless, pale gold. Girls' green and faded frocks
Are willow trees where burst out the unbridled birds.

Golden as a louis, lid warm and pure of an eye,
The Kingcup, just at prompt noon, from its tarnished mirror
Turns, jealous—your marriage faith, O Spouse!—to the sky
Gone gray in its own heat: the dear and rosebright sphere.

III.

Too upright, Madame in the nearby meadow lingers
Where Man-of-the-Earth snowfalls. Sunshade pinched in fingers
She tramples the flower clusters—proud, proud indeed—
Her children that lie in the blossoming grasses read

In their red morocco book. Look, alas! but he,
Like myriad white angels, split up en route, has started
To saunter off away beyond the mountain. She,
All cold and dark, still runs. After the male has parted.

IV.

Regrets for young arms, thick with the pure grass; for May
Moons, golden, deep inside the holy bed's own heart;
For joy of abandoned river lumberyards, prey
To August evenings where germs of this slow rot start.

For the while, let her weep beneath the ramparts; sighs
On high, of poplars, are the breeze, alone, for now.
Sourceless, reflectionless and gray, this surface lies
Where some old dredger toils in his unmoving scow.

V.

Toy in this eye of sorry water, I cannot reach—
My arms too short, my boat that its own mooring hinders!—
One flower or the other; the yellow that beseeches
There, nor the blue, friends, in this water gray as cinders.

What powder of the willow trees, shaken by one wing!
The roses of these reeds, devoured now, a long time!
My boat still standing with its drawn chain tightening
In this watery rimless eye—in what deep slime?

TRUE NAME

—Yves Bonnefoy

Desert, I'll call this castle which you were;
Night, I'll name this voice; Absence, this face;
And when you fall into the sterile earth,
That lightning which bore you here, Nothingness.

To die is a land you loved. I come
Only eternally by your dark ways.
I destroy your memory, desire, your form.
I am your foe who shall be pitiless.

I'll name you War and I shall take all fierce
Liberties of the war on you; I shall possess
Within my hands, your face, darkened and pierced,
Within my heart, this land, brightened by storm.

SAN FRANCESCO, AT NIGHT

—Yves Bonnefoy

And so, in that dark chamber, marble was the floor
On which you came, led on by Hope beyond all cure;
It might have been calm waters where redoubled lights
Bore far away the voice of candles and the night.

Yet, though, there was no ship there calling for a shore;
No footstep troubled the water's stillness now. And so
It is, I tell you, it is so with our other mirages. O
Festivals of our heart, torches which endure!

THE TOWNS

—Corrado Govoni

A sympathy of bells explodes
From a white bell-tower above
Gray roofs. Out of a huge oven
Women with red kerchiefs pull the loaves.

In the new snow they've brought a pig
To slaughter; around, enchanted by
The blood, children wait for that quick
Cruel agony, with big eyes.

The cocks all peal triumphantly.
Oxen come from the black hay-barns,
Spreading over the banksides, quietly,

Then go down, grave, to drink the silver water.
In the fields, pink and white, the graveyards
Shine among the green waves of the wheat.

DENK' ES, O SEELE

—Eduard Mörike

A pine seedling somewhere springs,
Within what woods, who knows?
In who can tell what garden
Some rosebush grows.
Already they are fated—
Remember it, my soul—
Into your grave to strike
Roots and to grow.

Two black colts graze
In open pastures, or
Homeward to the town,
Turn, lively and capering.
How slowly they will pace
Before your corpse,
Perhaps, perhaps before
They have worn loose
Upon their hooves those shoes
That I see glittering.

ON MY CHILD'S DEATH

—Joseph von Eichendorff,
Auf Meines Kindes Tod (8)

Clocks strike in the distance,
Already the night grows late,
How dimly the lamp glistens;
Your bed is all made.

It is the wind goes, only,
Grieving around the house;
Where, inside, we sit lonely
Often listening out.

It is as if, how lightly,
You must be going to knock,
Had missed your way and might be
Tired, now, coming back.

We are poor, poor stupid folk!
It's we, still lost in dread,
Who wander in the dark—
You've long since found your bed.

"ALS DU MICH EINST . . ."

—Rainer Maria Rilke

You found me, not so long ago
  When I was small, so small;
I bloomed, then, like a lindenbough
  Silent in you, that's all.

I was so small, I had no name
  And dwindled longingly
Until you said I was too great
  For any name to be.

I feel now I am one within
  Myth, May and the main sea;
Grown heavy as scent of wine within
  Your soul, now, that contains me.

SLUMBERSONG

—Rainer Maria Rilke

When I lose you, someday,
how will you sleep without me
whispering myself away
above you like the linden tree?

Without me waking to lay down
words, as close as eyelids,
upon your breasts, upon
your limbs, upon your lips?

Without my closing you to leave
you alone with what is yours,
like a garden with its sheaves
of melissas and of anise-stars.

DER PANTHER

Im Jardin des Plantes, Paris

—Rainer Maria Rilke

Always passing bars has dulled
His sight so, it will hold no more.
For him, there are a thousand bars;
Behind the thousand bars, no world.

The soft walk of his strong, lithe strides
Turns in the smallest of all orbits
Like the dance of force around an axis
Where a great will stands stupefied.

Only sometimes, the curtain of his eye
Lifts, noiselessly—an image enters,
That runs through his tense, arrested members
Into the heart, to die.

AN ARCHAIC TORSO OF APOLLO

—Rainer Maria Rilke

We will not ever know his legendary head
Wherein the eyes, like apples, ripened. Yet
His torso glows like a candelabra
In which his vision, merely turned down low,

Still holds and gleams. If this were not so, the curve
Of the breast could not so blind you, nor this smile
Pass lightly through the soft turn of the loins
Into that center where procreation flared.

If this were not so, this stone would stand defaced, maimed,
Under the transparent cascade of the shoulder,
Not glimmering that way, like a wild beast's pelt,

Nor breaking out of all its contours
Like a star; for there is no place here
That does not see you. You must change your life.

FROM RAINER MARIA RILKE

SONNETS TO ORPHEUS

I, 1

A tree rose up. O clear transcendency!
O Orpheus sings! A tall tree in the ear.
All things were hushed. Yet even silently
New origins, beckonings and change appear.
Creatures of silence crowded from the clear
Released wood out of burrow, den and lair.
It turned out they were not so hushed within
Themselves from cunning nor so stilled with fear

But with their listening. Bellow, shriek and roar
Seemed little in their hearts. And where had been
Scarcely a hut to take that in before,
A shelter, hidden from their dark desiring,
Having an entryway whose timbers tremble,—
You founded temples for them in their hearing.

I, 2

And nearly a girl it was, then, issuing
From this harmonious joy of song and lyre,
And shining clearly through her veils of Spring
She made herself a bed inside my ear.
And slept in me. And all things were her sleep.
The trees, that always had astonished me,
Tangible distances, the meadow felt,
Every wondering that had surprised my self.

She slept the world. How ever did you so
Achieve her, singing god, that she'd not long
To waken first? See, she arose and slept.
Where is her death? O find out this theme yet
Before your singing is consumed in song!—
Where does she sink from me . . . a girl almost . . .

I, 3

A god is able. But a mere man, through
The tight lyre, tell me, how can a man follow?
Your mind is cleavage. And wherever two
Heart roads cross, no temple stands to Apollo.
To sing by his schooling is not desire;
No courting something gotten in the end.
Singing is Being. And simple to *his* lyre.
But we, when *are* we? When does the god spend

Earth and all stars in our Being? Poet,
Youngster, it's not this, not your first love's care,
Although your mouth flew open. Learn to forget,
Forget the sudden singing. It will dwindle.
The real song is a different breath. An air
For nothing. Drifting in the god. A wind.

I, 4

O you who are tender, step now and then
Into the breath that does not notice you;
Touching your cheeks, let it be drawn in two
To tremble behind you and be one again.
You who are sound, O you who have the luck,
You who seem to be beginning hearts.
Bows for the darts and targets of the darts,
More endlessly shine the smiles that your tears have marked.

Never fear suffering. The heaviness—
You may return it to the earth's own weight;
The mountains are heavy, heavy the seas.
You could not sustain even the trees
Your childhood planted, long since grown too great.
Ah, but the breezes . . . O the spaciousness . . .

I, 5

Erect no gravestone to his memory;
Just let the rose bloom for his sake each year.
For it is Orpheus. His metamorphosis
In this one and this one. We needn't worry
For other names. Now and for all time
It's Orpheus when there's song. He comes and goes.
Isn't it much already if sometimes
He overstays, a few days, the bowl of roses?

For you to grasp it, he must disappear!
Though he, himself, takes fright at vanishing.
Even while his word exceeds existence here
He's gone already ways you cannot trace.
The lyre's lattice does not bind his hands.
Even in overstepping, he obeys.

I, 6

Does he come from here? No, from both realms
Has his broad nature grown.
More masterfully would he bend the willows' limbs
Who willows' roots had known.
On the table, leave, when you go to bed,
No bread or milk; it will draw the dead.
But him, the necromancer, let him blend,
Under the mildness of the eyelid,

Their aspect in the look of everything.
Let earthsmoke and mystery, in their magic,
Be true to him as the most mordant logic.
For him there must be nothing that can damage,
Whether from rooms or graves, the valid image;
Let him praise jug, clasp and finger-ring.

I, 7

Praising, that's it! Chosen to praise,
He came like ore out of the stone's
Silence. His heart, the ephemeral press
For men, of an eternal wine.
In the godlike example's grip
His voice does not fall into drought.
All turns vineyard, all turns grape,
Ripened in his sensitive South.

No mold in the Imperial Vaults
Gives the lie to his praising, nor
That from the gods a shadow falls.
He is one messenger who stays;
Who still holds into the door
Of the dead, bowls with fruits worth praise.

I, 8

Only in areas of Praise may walk
Mourning, nymph of the fountain wept,
To see that our downfall is kept
Clear even to the selfsame rock
That bears the gateways and the altars.
Look, the feeling she's the youngest one
Among the siblings of the spirit dawns
Just now around her quiet shoulders.

Rejoicing *knows*, Longing is compliant,—
Mourning alone still learns; like maidenhands
She counts up all night long the ancient curse.
Yet suddenly, aslant, unpracticed even,
She lifts a constellation of our voice,
Unclouded by her breath, into the Heavens.

I, 9

He only who has raised
Among the shadows, too, his lyre,
Foretells and can restore
Unceasing praise.
Who with the dead has eaten
Their poppy, he alone
Will never lose again
The lightest tone.

Though the reflection in the pool
Often before our eyes is swimming,
Know the image.
Nowhere but in the dual
Kingdom shall a voice become
Everlasting, calm.

I, 10

Antique sarcophagi, who have stayed
Always in my emotions, I greet you,
Whom jubilant waters of the Roman days,
Like a wandering song, flow through.
Or those, the opened ones, like eyes
Of some awakening, glad shepherd
—Full of silence and the bee-sucked herbs—
Where fluttered the enchanted butterflies.

All that a man extracts from doubt
I greet, the once more opening mouths
That knew already what the silence meant.
Do *we* know, friends, or do we not?
The lingering hour molds them both
Into the face of man.

II, 4

(The Tapestry of the Lady with the Unicorn)

O this is the beast that does not have being!
But they did not know that. And then besides,
—The neck, the strong stance, the decisive strides,
And even to the still light of its seeing
—They loved it. And because they loved it (Indeed,
It never *was*), a pure creature happened.
They allowed room, left always clear and opened,
Where it easily raised its head and had scarce need

To be. They fed it on no oats nor corn
But only on the chance it might be. Might.
Fodder that gave such force to the creature
It drove a horn out of its brow. One horn.
Then to a virgin came here, trotting white,—
Was in the silver-mirror and in her.

ABOUT THE AUTHOR

W. D. SNODGRASS was born in Beaver Falls, Pennsylvania, and was educated at Geneva College and the State University of Iowa. He has taught English at Cornell, Rochester and Wayne State University; he is presently at Syracuse University. Mr. Snodgrass was a grantee of the National Institute of Arts and Letters and has received a fellowship in poetry from the *Hudson Review.* His previous collection of poetry, *Heart's Needle,* won the Pulitzer Prize in 1960.

Format by Katharine Sitterly

Set in Intertype Weiss

Composed and printed by York Composition Co., Inc.

Bound by The Haddon Craftsmen, Inc.

HARPER & ROW, PUBLISHERS, INCORPORATED